D1458603

Advice on
Courtship
&
Marriage

Emily Jessop

summersdale

ADVICE ON COURTSHIP AND MARRIAGE

Summersdale Publishers Ltd
46 West Street
Chichester
West Sussex
PO19 1RP
UK

www.summersdale.com

Printed and bound in China

ISBN: 978-1-84024-773-2

Substantial discounts on bulk quantities of Summersdale books are available to corporations, professional associations and other organisations. For details telephone Summersdale Publishers on (+44-1243-771107), fax (+44-1243-786300) or email (nicky@summersdale.com).

Advice on
Courtship
&
Marriage

Emily Jessop

ADVICE AND INSTRUCTION FOR LADIES AND GENTLEMEN OF SOCIETY

on the Conduct and Procedure of Courtship and Marriage in keeping with the Greater Spiritual Sanctity and Moral Well-Being of Both Sexes

Court Scientifically

If you court at all, court scientifically. Bungle whatever else you will, but do not bungle courtship. A failure in this may mean more than a loss of wealth or public honours; it may mean ruin, or a life often worse than death.

Good Behaviour

A young lady should not permit her gentlemen friends to address her by her home name, and the reverse is true. Use the title Miss and Mr respectively.

A gentleman should never use the term 'Dear' or 'My Dear' under any circumstances unless he knows it is perfectly acceptable or a long and friendly acquaintance justifies it.

Court Purely

All men feel much better for going a courting, providing they court purely. Nothing tears the life out of man more than lust, vulgar thoughts and immoral conduct.

Nearly all this wide-spread crime and suffering connected with public and private licentiousness and prostitution, has its origin in these unmeaning courtships – every young man who courts without intending to marry, is throwing himself or his sweet-heart into this hell upon earth.

The Best Time

All things considered, we advise the male reader to keep his desires in check till he is at least twenty-five, and the female not to enter the pale of wedlock until she has attained the age of twenty.

A young couple should first carefully learn each other by making the courtship a matter of business, and sufficiently long that the disposition and temper of each may be thoroughly exposed and understood.

Upon First Acquaintance

A lady, be she young or old, never forms an acquaintance upon the streets or seeks to attract the attention or admiration of persons of the other sex. To do so would render false her claims to her ladyhood, if it did not make her liable to far graver charges.

Never make acquaintances in coffee-houses or other public places. As no person who respects himself does so, you may reasonably suspect any advances made to you.

Where to Date

Keep away from the moral pesthouses. The music, singing and dancing are simply a blind to cover the intemperance and lust, which hold high carnival in these gilded hells.

A Tempered Match

Keep the company of those ladies who awaken your higher sentiments and nobler impulses, in whose presence you would no more feel your passions aroused than in the presence of your own mother.

Receiving Calls

A young lady who is not engaged may receive calls and attention from such unmarried gentlemen as she desires, and may accept invitation to ride, to concerts, to theatres, etc.

A lady never calls on a gentleman, unless professionally or officially. It is not only ill-bred, but positively improper to do so.

Receiving the Attentions of Gentlemen

No well bred lady will too eagerly receive the attentions of a gentleman, no matter how much she admires him; nor, on the other hand, will she be so reserved as to altogether discourage him.

A lady never demands attentions and favours from a gentleman, but always accepts them gratefully and graciously and with expressed thanks. Unmarried ladies should not accept presents from gentlemen to whom they are neither related nor engaged.

A young lady should not allow special attention from anyone to whom she is not specially attracted.

It is only the contemptible flirt that keeps an honourable man in suspense for the purpose of glorifying herself by his attentions in the eyes of friends. Nor would any but a frivolous or vicious girl boast of the offer she has received and rejected.

Up and At It

Dress up, spruce up, and be on the alert. Don't wait too long to get one much more perfect than you are; but settle on some one soon.

Bad Dressing

If women knew how much mischief they do men they would change some of their habits of dress. The dress of their busts, the padding in different parts, are so contrived as to call away attention from the soul and fix it on the bosom and hips.

Appropriate Attire

Avoid what is called the 'ruffianly style of dress' or the slouchy appearance of a half-unbuttoned vest, and suspenderless pantaloons. That sort of affectation is, if possible, even more disgusting than the painfully elaborate frippery of the dandy or dude.

Be Self-supporting

The young man who gives evidence of thrift is always in demand. Be enthusiastic and drive with success all that you undertake. Woman admires a certainty.

On Exercise

How many English girls who live in London and other large towns ever take any exercise worth speaking of, outside the ball-room? It is true they visit Regent Street often enough, as many a cheque-book will show; but in most instances they drive there, and afterwards drive home with the conviction that they have walked quite far enough to tire themselves, whereas in truth it is not the walking that has tired them, but the standing so long at the shop windows and in the shops.

Etiquette of the Ballroom

Certain persons are appointed to act as stewards whose office it is to see that every thing be conducted in a proper manner: if you are entirely a stranger, it is to them you must apply for a partner, and point out (quietly) any young lady with whom you would like to dance... do not, on any account, go to a strange lady by yourself and request her to dance, as she will unhesitatingly 'decline the honour', and think you an impertinent fellow for your presumption.

Dancing

Any presentation to a lady in a public ball-room, for the mere purpose of dancing, does not entitle you to claim her acquaintance afterwards; therefore, should you meet her the next day, do not attempt to address her. At most, you may lift you hat; but even that is better avoided – unless, indeed, she first bow – as neither she nor her friends know *who* or *what* you are.

The Rejected Partner

If a lady should civilly decline to dance with you, making an excuse, and you chance to see her dancing afterwards, do not take any notice of it, nor be offended with her. It might not be that she despised you, but that she preferred another. We cannot always fathom the hidden springs which influence a woman's actions.

Escorting a Lady Home

When a gentleman escorts a lady home from a ball, she should not invite him to enter the house; and even if she does so, he should by all means decline the invitation.

You should offer your arm to a lady with whom you are walking whenever her safety, comfort or convenience may seem to require such attention on your part.

Looking Upon a Lady

A well-bred man always removes his cigar from his lips whenever he bows to a lady. No gentleman will stand in the doors of hotels, nor on the corners of the street, gazing impertinently at the ladies as they pass. That is such an unmistakable sign of a loafer, that one can hardly imagine a well-bred man doing such a thing.

Etiquette of a Dinner Party

Never pare an apple or a pear for a lady unless she desire you, and then be careful to use your fork to hold it: you may sometimes offer to divide a very large pear with a person, or for them.

Do not ask a lady to take wine, until you see she has finished her fish or soup.

Table Manners

Ladies should never dine with their gloves on – unless their hands are not fit to be seen.

It is not too much to say, that a young woman who elected to take claret with her fish, or eat peas with her knife, would justly run the risk, the punishment, of being banished from good society.

Conversation

In talking with ladies of ordinary education, avoid political, scientific, or commercial topics, and choose only such subjects as are likely to be of interest to them. Do not use a classical quotation in the presence of ladies without apologising for, or translating it.

One does not wish to hear a lady talk politics nor a smattering of science; but she should be able to understand and listen with interest when politics are discussed, and to appreciate, in some degree, the conversation of scientific men.

Speaking Correctly

Remember that all 'slang' is vulgar. It has become of late unfortunately prevalent, and we have known even ladies pride themselves on the saucy chique with which they adopt certain cant phrases of the day.

A gentleman should never permit any phrase that approaches to an oath, to escape his lips in the presence of a lady.

The Young Woman's Caution

Let no young lady ever once think of bestowing her affections till she is certain they will not be broken off – that is, until the match is fully agreed upon, but rather let her keep her heart whole till she bestows it for life.

Improper Liberties

Any improper liberties which are permitted by young ladies, whether engaged or not, will change love into sensuality, and her affections will become obnoxious, if not repellent.

Sensuality will drive away the roses in the cheeks of womanhood, undermine health and produce a brazen countenance that can be read by all men.

Ruinous Passion

A young man who allows his mind to dwell upon the vision of nude women will soon become a victim of ruinous passion.

To a gentleman seeking a partner for life, we would say look to it, that you be not entrapped by a beautiful face.

A Sure Remedy for Heartbreak

Come in contact with the other sex. You are infused with your lover's magnetism, which must remain till displaced by another's.

Go to parties and picnics; be free, familiar, offhand, even forward; try your knack at fascinating another, and yield to fascinations yourself. But be honest, command respect and make yourself attractive and worthy.

Cultivate Deficiencies

Men and women poorly sexed treat each other with more or less indifference, whereas a hearty sexuality inspires both to a right estimation of the faculties and qualities of each other.

Distrust and Want of Confidence

Most difficulties arise from distrust or lack of confidence or common-sense. When two lovers eye each other like two curs, each watching, lest the other should gain some new advantage, then this shows a lack of common-sense, and the young couple should get sensible or separate.

Proximity of the Sexes

The close personal proximity of the sexes is greatly undesirable before marriage. Kisses and caresses are most properly the monopoly of wives. Such indulgences have a direct and powerful physiological effect. Nay, they often lead to the most fatal results.

The Dangers of Promiscuity

The young man who may take pleasure in the fact that he is the hero of half a dozen or more engagements and love episodes, little realises that such constant excitement often causes dangerously frequent and long-continued nocturnal emissions.

Young man, beware; your punishment for trifling with the affections of others may cost you a life of affliction.

Visiting Hours

No young man should ever prolong his visits beyond ten o'clock… unless it be the common custom of the family to remain up and to entertain visitors to a later hour… Two hours is quite long enough for a call.

Very few young men comprehend the real pain and inconvenience they occasion to the lady of their choice when they keep her up to untoward hours, and subject her, in consequence, to the ridicule and censure of others.

Early Marriages

Women too early married always remain small in stature, weak, pale, emaciated, and more or less miserable.

Whom to Choose for a Husband

The choice of a husband requires the coolest judgment and the most vigilant sagacity.

Caution

If a young man is indifferent to his sisters he will become indifferent to his wife as soon as the honey moon is over.

Don't marry an intemperate man with a view of reforming him. Thousands have tried it and failed. Misery, sorrow and a very hell on earth have been the consequences of too many such generous undertakings.

The Woman Who Makes the Best Wife

She who is brainy enough to be a companion, wise enough to be a counsellor, skilled enough in the domestic virtues to be a good housekeeper, and loving enough to guide in true paths the children with whom the home may be blessed.

She should have no 'career', or desire for a career, if she would fill to perfection the home sphere.

Safe Hints

Bright red hair should marry jet black, and jet black auburn or bright red, etc. And the more red-faced and bearded or impulsive a man, the more dark, calm, cool and quiet should his wife be; and vice versa. Red-whiskered men should marry brunettes, but not blondes; the colour of the whiskers being more determinate of the temperament than that of the hair.

Small, nervous men must not marry little, nervous or sanguine women, lest both they and their children have quite too much of the hot-headed and impulsive, and die suddenly.

Society, Rules and Customs

To keep a lady's company six months is a public announcement of an engagement.

It is very injudicious, not to say presumptuous, for a gentleman to make a proposal to a young lady on too brief acquaintance. A lady who would accept a gentleman at first sight can hardly possess the discretion needed to make a good wife.

Upon Proposing

If a young man is very bashful, he should write his sentiments in a clear, frank manner on a neat white sheet of note paper, enclose it in a plain white envelope and find some way to convey it to the lady's hand.

It is customary in polite society for the young man to affix the seal of this engagement by some present to his affianced. This present is usually a ring… and as expensive as the young man's means will justify.

It is not always necessary to take a lady's first refusal as absolute. Diffidence or uncertainty as to her own feelings may sometimes influence a lady to reply in the negative, and after consideration cause her to regret that reply.

Though a gentleman may repeat his suit with propriety after having been once repulsed, still it should not be repeated too often nor too long, lest it should degenerate into importuning.

On Engagements

But protracted courtship, or engagements, are if possible, to be avoided; they are universally embarrassing.

When a couple become engaged, the gentleman presents the lady with a ring, which is worn on the ring-finger of the right hand. He may also make her other small presents from time to time, until they are married, but if she has any scruples about accepting them, he can send her flowers, which are at all times acceptable.

Benefits of Marriage

Marriage purifies the complexion, removes blotches from the skin, invigorates the body, fills up the tones of the voice, gives elasticity and firmness to the step.

Statistics show that married men live longer than bachelors. Child-bearing for women is conducive to longevity.

A Good Husband

He will allow his life-companion a bank account, and will exact no itemised bill at the end of the month. Above all, he will pay the Easter bonnet bill without a word, never bring a friend to dinner without first telephoning home.

The Wedding Day

She will understand that it is to her advantage to select a wedding day about fifteen or eighteen days after the close of menstruation in the month chosen, since it is not best that the first child should be conceived during the excitement or irritation of first attempts at congress; besides modest brides naturally do not wish to become large with child before the season of congratulation and visiting on their return from the 'wedding tour' is over.

The Honeymoon

If the Conventional Tour is taken, the husband should remember that his bride cannot stand the same amount of tramping around and sight-seeing that he can. The female organs of generation are so easily affected by excessive exercise of the limbs which support them, that at this critical period it would be a foolish and costly experience to drag a lady hurriedly around the country. In many cases it lays the foundation for the wife's first and life-long 'backache'.

Becoming a Husband

When a man marries, it is understood that all former acquaintanceship *ends*...

A bachelor is seldom very *particular* in the choice of his companions. So long as he is amused, he will associate freely enough with those whose morals and habits would point them out as highly dangerous persons to introduce into the sanctity of domestic life.

Last Meal

When a man is about to be married, he usually gives a dinner to his bachelor friends; which is understood to be their congé, unless he choose to renew their acquaintance.

Inequality of the Sexes

It is no slander to say that many men have wives much more refined than themselves. This is natural in the inequalities of life.

How often the spell of beauty is broken by coarse, loud talking! In the social circle how pleasant it is to hear a woman talk in that low key which always characterises the true lady! In the sanctuary of home how such a voice soothes the fretful temper and cheers the weary husband!

Moral Relations

The moral relations existing between the married couple undergo unfortunate changes; this affection, founded upon reciprocal esteem, is little by little effaced by the repetition of an act which pollutes the marriage bed.

No wife should indulge her husband when he is under the influence of alcoholic stimulants, for idiocy and other serious maladies are liable to be visited upon the offspring.

On a Husband's Character

Study your husband's character – he has his peculiarities. Consult his tastes. It is more important to your home that you should please him than anybody else.

A man will make a comrade of the woman who stimulates him to higher achievement, but he will love the one who makes herself a mirror for his conceit.

At Home and Abroad

Never let your husband have cause to complain that you are more agreeable abroad than at home; nor permit him to see in you an object of admiration as respects your dress and manners, when in company, while you are negligent of both in the domestic circle.

No wife acts wisely who permits her sitting-room to look dull in the eyes of him whom she ought especially to please, and with whom she has to pass her days.

Master Your Own Temper

If small disputes arise, and your wife has not sufficient good sense to yield her opinion... do not get angry; rather be silent and let the matter rest. An opportunity will soon occur of speaking affectionately, yet decidedly, on the subject, and much good will be affected. Master your own temper, and you will soon master your wife's.

Souvenirs of Bachelor Days

The woman who finally acquires legal possession of a man is haunted by the shadowy predecessors. One by one, the cherished souvenirs of his bachelor days disappear. Pictures painted by rival fair ones go to adorn the servant's room, through gradual retirement backward. Rare china is mysteriously broken. Sofa cushions never 'harmonise with the tone of the room', and the covers have to be changed.

It takes time, but usually by the first anniversary of a man's marriage, his penates have been nobly weeded out, and the things he has left are of his wife's choosing, generously purchased with his own money.

On Courtship Within the Marriage

If women did not demand so much, men in general would be more thoughtful. If it were understood that even after marriage man was still to be the lover, the one who sent roses to his sweetheart would sometimes bring them to his wife. The pretty courtesies would not so often be forgotten.

It seems to be a settled thing that men shall do the courting before marriage and women afterward.

A Perfect Match

The best wife is the woman who has found the right husband, a husband who understands her. A man will have the best wife when he rates that wife as queen among women. This sort of man will not only praise the dishes made by his wife, but will actually eat them.

Provenance of Material

All the material used in this book was adapted from the following sources:

Day, C. W. M., *Hints on Etiquette and the Usages of Society with a Glance at Bad Habits* (1834, Turnstile Press)

Jeffries, B. J., & Nichols, J. L., *Searchlights on Health* (1920, J. L. Nichols & Co.)

Mackarness, H., *The Young Ladies Book* (1888, Routledge)

Reed, M., *The Spinster Book*, (1901, The Knickerbocker Press)

Ruth, J. A., & Co., *The Rules of Etiquette: Decorum: A Practical Treatise on Etiquette and Dress of the Best American Society* (1877, J. A Ruth & Co.)

Young, J. H., *Our Deportment: The Manners, Conduct and Dress of the Most Refined Society* (1881, Union Publishing House)

Have you enjoyed this book? If so, why not
write a review on your favourite website?

Thanks very much for buying
this Summersdale book.

www.summersdale.com